THE SOUL OF THE ISSACHAR SEER

Ken Cox

Copyright © 2020 by Ken Cox

All rights reserved. No part of this publication may be reproduced, distributed or transmitted in any form or by any means, including photocopying, recording, or other electronic or mechanical methods, without the prior written permission of the publisher, except in the case of brief quotations embodied in critical reviews and certain other noncommercial uses permitted by copyright law. For permission requests, write to the publisher, addressed "Attention: Permissions Coordinator," at the address below.

Ken Cox /Rejoice Essential Publishing
PO BOX 512
Effingham, SC 29541
www.republishing.org

Unless otherwise indicated, scriptures are taken from the King James Version.

Scripture quotations marked (NIV) are taken from the Holy Bible, New International Version®, NIV®. Copyright © 1973, 1978, 1984, 2011 by Biblica, Inc.™ Used by permission of Zondervan. All rights reserved worldwide. www.zondervan.comThe "NIV" and "New International Version" are trademarks registered in the United States Patent and Trademark Office by Biblica, Inc.™

The Soul of The Issachar Seer/Ken Cox
ISBN-13: 978-1-952312-33-5
Library of Congress Control Number: 2020917468

TABLE OF CONTENTS

INTRODUCTION..1

CHAPTER 1:   The Issue with the
               Prophets Soul.....................4

CHAPTER 2:   Developing the Inner
               Life of the
               Seer / Prophet...................13

CHAPTER 3:   Awakening the
               Spiritual Senses.................20

CHAPTER 4:   Dealing with
               the Blindness of
               the Prophets Soul..............28

CHAPTER 5:   The Stronghold
               of the Soul of a Seer.........38

CHAPTER 6:   Seeking and Training
               for The
               Issachar Anointing.............47

CHAPTER 7:   The Eschatology
               of a Prophet's

	Tormented Soul..................58
CHAPTER 8:	The Power of The Issachar Prophets Spoken Word....................70
CHAPTER 9:	How Do I Get The Issachar Anointing Upon My Life...................78
CHAPTER 10:	History of The Issachar Anointing............85

ABOUT THE AUTHOR..95

INTRODUCTION

Here we are in another generation, once we were the children of leaders and now we've become leaders. Let us assume that we have accepted our calls in life, and we are active as seers. We are all different; the patterns of our lives have taken us in different places and directions. We must be empowered but we must also be ready individually. Therefore, focus on the soul is critical for every seer.

This book will focus on developing the soul of an aspiring 'Issachar Seer.' According to the Scripture, this prophet was known to be astute in times and seasons. The type of prophet who aspires to this mantle will come to understand the importance of development. The opportunity for us to accomplish the purposes of God is simply priceless for any prophet to be effective and relevant, and the Issachar Seer is no exception.

My personal goal is to empower prophets as well as myself. I love to grow in my calling. Growth prepares us for our ultimate placement of God as He moves us to our destiny. We all have a destiny and to walk into it should be our ultimate purpose in His service.

My special prayer for hungry prophetic readers of this book is that you are genuinely empowered by understanding that your soul must be in a certain order, and in place to function at the highest level for Gods' purposes. Today, the Issachar prophet/seer represents a much needed generational prophetic office.

My prayer is that you feel as compelled as I do, as we are called to walk as vessels of a much needed prophetic movement. You will see that I will focus on the soul, the needed connection to the spirit and how we can become relevant Issachar seers. Our souls need work, plain and simple. Are you ready for this uncommon journey?

I welcome you to walk with me as I dedicate this book to the multitude of aspiring prophets who seek God for more. You are my kind of prophets. We all need a check within the soul. This is my offering to you to help identify and develop the soul for the 'Issachar Anointing' of a prophet.

We are in a special season, which has sneaked upon so many of us, we find ourselves unprepared or at a loss for direction. Today, there is a loss of prophetic edge. We can discern, but we desperately need to recover the edge back to our mantles. Thanks for allowing me to share this revelation with you.

CHAPTER 1

THE ISSUE WITH THE PROPHETS SOUL

Allow me to take this step by step just- as God gave it to me. I will start with the basic makeup of our soul in this chapter. The soul of a prophet consists of three parts. The mind, the will, and the emotions. Proverbs 2:10 (NIV) says, "Wisdom will enter your heart, and knowledge will be pleasant to your soul." Let us now know that knowledge is a matter of the mind, and the mind is an intimate member of the soul. Lamentations 3:20 says, "My Soul remembers them well," so the soul of a prophet is active. As I use the term prophet, rest assured I am talking about Prophets and Apostles, Seers, Watchmen, and the 5-fold ministry gifts who are prophetically gifted.

Let's look at Job 7:15 says, "My Soul would choose," and 6:7 says, "My soul refuses." To choose and to refuse are both decisions and functions of the will. The will of a prophet is part of a prophet's soul. 1st Chronicles 22:19 says, "Now set your heart and your soul to seek after Jehovah your God."

A prophet's emotions comprise many things including: love, hatred, joy, and grief. Song of Songs 1:7 and Psalm 42:1 shows us that to love is a function of the soul. 2nd Samuel 5:8, Psalm 107:18, and Ezekiel 36:5 shows us that hating, loathing, and despising are also in the soul. Despising in the soul is the hatred of the soul. These are emotions, and they are a part of the prophet's soul.

So now that we had a review, these three parts of our soul allow us to look at ourselves. This affords us the chance to understand why it is so important to the prophet that we know ourselves. 1st Corinthians 4:1-2 says, "Let a man so account of us, as of the ministers of Christ, and stewards of God's mysteries. Moreover, it is required in stewards that a man is found faithful." We, the prophets of God, are the stewards of God. We are the maintainers of His Word.

Because we are the maintainers of His Word, we need to apply 3 John 2. It says, "Beloved, I wish above all things that thou mayest prosper and be in health, even as thy soul prospereth." Prophets get this key; Prosperity is a Soul issue and not a spiritual issue. The question every prophet must ask is if your soul is prospering. Is your mind, will, and emotions in line with God's Word?

Most prophets are doing Spiritual warfare, but we need some soul warfare. My soul must employ a healthy submission for God's prosperity to be upon us. Our health is tied to this and we, the prophets, are not in tune with what is happening with our souls.

What is blocking our soul's prosperity is keeping us broke busted and disgusted, and our health in a continual spiral of dysfunction. Psalms 139:14 says that my soul knoweth right well. My soul has been educated by my spirit. My soul must submit to the Spirit for me to be educated. Prophet, you have given yourself to God, understand that the attacks you are under are spiritual, but they are focused toward your soul. This is where your confusion is located.

When my Spirit has not educated my soul, or my soul refuses revelation knowledge then I should be able to see why as a prophet, I do not walk in prosperity. 2 Chronicles 20:20 says, "Believe in the Word of God so shall you be established, believe in his prophet, so shall you prosper."

We must know as prophets that our soul is prospering, or we will be non-effective, irrelevant people will believe in us and they will be highly disappointed because we were parading around as something we are not. The main reason is that we find ourselves often unteachable. Psalms 103 outlines that we must pay attention to our soul. Verses 1-2 says to "Bless the Lord, O my Soul: and all that is within me, bless his holy name. Bless the Lord, O my Soul, and forget not all his benefits."

Did you ever notice the emphasis is on the soul and what it needs to do? The soul must come in line with the Word of God, Prophet. We do not have a prosperity problem; we have a soul problem. The soul is blocked from communicating. This signals an attack on our souls. The enemy has done his level best to make you, the prophet of God, ineffective because the enemy has attacked your Soul.

Sure, we have been talking, proclaiming the Word of God, speaking in the name of Jesus, but the reality is that most of us have not understood the status of our soul. So here we are ministering to people, but we, the prophets, have soul issues.

Psalms 35:27 makes us look at ourselves even as closely as it says, "Let them shout for joy, and be glad, that favor my righteous cause: yea, let them say continually, Let the Lord be magnified, which hath pleasure in the prosperity of his servant." Ok, we know this Scripture to be true then why do so many of us have a problem when God displays prosperity through a man or a woman of God?

God shows us a breakthrough anointing, and we are too blind to see it. We will drag a prophet's name through the mud, attack his or her ministry and go out of our way to degrade them, all because we have made an obvious decision to live in poverty. Or are we still teaching, preaching, and denigrating our peers because God blesses them?

Prophet, what will bear witness with your Spirit? The Word of God for so many of us has not born witness because of how we dishonor our prophetic peers, prophetic mentors, and leaders. Jeremiah 33:9 says, "And it shall be to me a name of joy, a praise and an honor before all the nations of the earth, which shall hear all the good that I do unto them: and they shall fear and tremble for all the goodness and for all the prosperity that I procure unto it." This Scripture must bother prophets and people alike who do not feel or understand that our soul needs special attention.

To get a handle on this, let's realize that Satan has built a stronghold on prosperity in many of our minds, wills, and emotions. The strongholds are fixed and stable until we never get the understanding or mentorship in those areas, so we go about life trying to understand why the Word of God is ineffective in our lives. The problem is us, the prophet, with our individual hang-ups, the problem is not God, again the problem is us.

We have allowed ourselves to think and function with these strongholds, and we have not considered that we have been in the way of our prosperity and the prosperity of others who are assigned to us, Prophet. Our souls have not been aligned right.

A prophet's personal stronghold must be pulled down. Then submission, totally on the Word of God must be enforced to deal with future attacks. Notice that this issue is in your soul, not your spirit. The mind, the will, and the emotions are the components of the soul.

Start right now: curse the stronghold on your life in Jesus' name. Do it now as you read this prophet, as you realize you just caught a thief. That thief will no longer block your blessings. Watch God move even now as you repeat it, curse the stronghold, right now in the name of Jesus. Curse the stronghold on your finances, health, children, grandchildren, godchildren, spiritual children, family, and spouse. Curse and break the strongholds now in every area of your life in the name of Jesus.

Know it now that you are going to be restored in every area of your life. What has not worked will work because you now understand that your soul must prosper and the transfer God has for you through your spirit is not blocked anymore by a thief that wants you to be confused and misunderstood in discerning his motives or his demonic operations.

Psalms 143:3-6 says, "For the enemy hath persecuted my soul; he hath smitten my life down to the ground; he hath made me to dwell in darkness, as those that have been long dead. Therefore is my Spirit overwhelmed within me; my heart within me is desolate. I remember the days of old; I meditate on all thy works; I muse on the work of thy hands. I stretch forth my hands unto thee: my Soul thirsteth after thee, as a thirsty land. Selah." Again, prophets, the issue is our soul, and we must remember it.

Our spirits are failing because our souls are blocked to what God is sending us. We, the prophets, are in a broken place. Understand that messages from God, travel through our spirit to our soul. When that channel of communication is blocked or held up, we are between a rock and a hard place. Our ability to function as prophets is stopped and extremely limited at the absolute best.

Psalms 143:7 says, "Hear me speedily, O Lord: my Spirit faileth: hide not thy face from me, lest I be like unto them that go down into the pit." Again, look at 3 John 2, which says, "Beloved, I wish above all things that thou mayest prosper and be in health, even as thy soul prospereth." We must learn that prosperity in any form is a Soul issue and not a spiritual issue. This includes our development as Seers. Again every prophet must ask him or herself if their soul is prospering. Prophet is your mind, will, and emotions in line with God's plans and His purposes?

People have a right to expect the highest reality of the calling as they sow into the prophetic gift. Your responsibility, Prophet, is to align your soul correctly so that the flow of the anointing can and will more freely. When we consider the reality of our Spirit and our Souls, which one needs the faith of God? The answer is easy; it is your soul. Look at us, and you will see that doubt, disbelief, and lack of commitment do not exist in the Spirit. They exist in our soul. We must mature and move to the place where our spirit, soul, and body move as one aligned unit.

Prophets must understand that the enemy will attack your soul, not your spirit. You must protect your soul with the sword of the Spirit. Destroy the works of the enemy by declaring and releasing the benefits of God by declaring His Word. Therefore, you must know God and know what His Word says so you can release it upon yourself. As your mind, will and emotions prosper, you will see the benefits upon your life.

How many prophets have quit releasing the Word of God upon themselves? Have you ever wondered why you have a word for everybody else and never a word for yourself? Something is wrong when the prophet who will not submit to the Word of God, but wants to be known for giving the very thing to which you will not submit.

Soul Prosperity is a full-time endeavor, which will automatically affect our health, finances, all areas of life. God has called you as a prophet to live how? 1. Not enough? 2. Just enough? Or 3. More than enough? The answer is obvious. Prophets, the spirit of poverty has held us down for too long, and if we are going to be the curse breakers, we have work to do. We must first do the work involved with the soul. Now that you have been with me for one chapter, allow me to expand on this as we talk about the inner life of a prophet.

CHAPTER 2

DEVELOPING THE INNER LIFE OF THE SEER/ PROPHET

There is a difference between Moses and almost all the prophets who followed him. Moses was familiar with God's plan and saw each prophetic assignment within the context of that plan. Today, as prophets, we struggle to understand the details of God's plan. Today's prophets seem to attempt to deduce the wider implications of God's master plan. Moses understood specific details because his soul was in harmony with his inner man or spirit man.

Why was Moses accorded the distinction of being the greatest and most special prophet of God ever? Let us look at his life because it starts with a marriage of his soul and inner man. Moses was probably the humblest man on earth. His mind was in the right place with God, and he did not view himself highly. Moses had no ego, and his mind was submitted to the plan of God.

God shows us a picture of our journey towards this "more excellent way" when we observe the Tabernacle of Moses. Exodus 25 refers to the tabernacle that was built in the wilderness after God delivered His people from Egypt. We journey into the tabernacle as prophets of God. This is a reflection on the soul (mind, will, emotions) of Moses, as he was a committed vessel of God.

Prophets: to begin, let's understand that the tabernacle is composed of the Outer Court. There is also the Inner Court (also called the Holy Place), and the Most Holy Place (also called the Holy of Holies). The Holy Place or the Holy of Holies are both covered under the same tent. This is referred to as the Tent of Testimony or Tent of the Congregation.

This place symbolizes those who abide in the Inner Courts of God, who will become a true testimony with true unity in brotherly love. This is what Moses did with his life. He gave God everything, literally everything. Inside this tent and the inner man, God wants every part of your life! Your soul is a critical part that needs to line up with your personal tabernacle that God will operate in.

This is a picture of us as we accept Jesus Christ into our hearts, and when we follow Him. Let us look at the tabernacle: we see white walls that represent the "Righteousness of God in Christ" surrounding the tabernacle. Imagine us, the prophets of God, we are righteous in Christ Jesus as the New Testament declares. Whether you act like it or not does not change this fact; however, following the "more excellent way" of God will cause you to walk in this fact. In our mind we have a powerful tool.

This is a difficult reality. Our inner man (spirit man) has become righteous by faith in Jesus even though the soul man was still quite the same as the day before. (I will discuss this more in The Eschatology of the Seer's soul chapter). The soul man still knew little of God's way.

This is us prophets! We learn how to yield to Christ. Christ has been accepted into our hearts, and yet there are many areas of our heart where we have not allowed Him. We profess, but we do not live it. The difference was that Moses allowed God to become the master of those areas. He did this by submission of his soul to God.

Prophet, this is the demonstration that all areas of our life must be dealt with. Moses shows us that one area cannot remain that stays undealt with, for God's Word goes forth to bring all areas into subjection. Every area of your life must become a testimony. Every area of your life must reflect the unity we have with walking with God in His garden.

Moses progressed in the "more excellent way" analogy. Every Prophet should not be content to abide outside of the tabernacle where the world assembles in the outer court. The Outer Court should be viewed only as a "passing through" area. When we enter the Holy Place, we see the great veil that divides us from the Holy of Holies. The Holy Place will bring the Prophet to a place of unity and testimony.

Now we can say when a Prophet's soul abides in the Holy of Holies then the inner man walks in a repentant state. Moses' life is an example of this. Moses walking in total obedience to the will of God and His obedience to the Word matured him and will mature us to become fruit. This is a fruit that shall be permanent.

The difference today is that many prophets did not see themselves this way. We all seem to want to achieve full communion with God, but we have not, and the question is why? I came to understand something about Moses. Moses was, in his consciousness, never overwhelmed. What am I saying? He could think he could process and his mind was open to the words God spoke to him. Can you say submission totally?

Even in our prophetic duties, God is more concerned with the messenger than the message? If the prophet is wrong, the prophetic message will be wrong too. Can you see why we must embody the message more than that we preserve our reputation as prophets? God will handle everything else. 1 John 4:1 tells us the Body of Christ must "test the spirits to see whether they are from God."

"The fruit we bear in the prophetic ministry comes as a natural by-product of our roots abiding in the relationship with God." 1 Corinthians 14:1 says that we are to desire earnestly spiritual gifts but especially prophecy. The Prophet Isaiah referred to the prophets as the eyes of Israel (Isaiah 29:10). Prophets can "see" things on a regular basis that others do not. Prophets have absolutely no power. The Holy Spirit's power must do all that is accomplished as we connect with our inner man that has been aligned with our soul. Remember, we are free moral agents, so our soul in this process is critical.

Think about this: as we mature, we become convinced of the value of the prophetic ministry. This becomes apparent in our personal lives and in the Body of Christ. We move into a state of being relevant. Once Moses was convinced, he became the preeminent Prophet of God and of his time. How did Moses know his mind was free from the fear of man? This is a question that will be answered as we examine his soul.

Moses, many times was a stranger among his own people. His mind was God-centered, and his people struggled to have an identity. It is a small wonder Moses did not go crazy around the people he was sent to save. The people who many times did not seem to have a clue and looked at him as a bigger problem than Pharaoh.

Moses, as we examine his soul (mind, will, and emotions), knew how much God loved him. Why is that important? John 5:44 helps us to know that our Heavenly Father's love produces rest for our soul. This allows us as Prophets to flow prophetically out of an overflow on a regular basis, and thus we avoid worn-out prophetic utterances that we hear repeatedly. God is a communicator with His prophets and has an abundance of things to say if we will learn His mode of operation.

Here now is where we start to explore the work needed to produce a functioning Issachar Seer. Moses gives us clues. Just like the Issachar prophets who were individuals of wisdom, counsel, insight, discipline, prophets today need to understand that our training is in life, and in the classroom (School of the Prophets and related events.)

The "inner man" or "spirit man" develops when the mind of the prophet is unoccupied by the cares of walking in consciousness, like Moses and the Issachar prophets. The soul is at rest, untroubled by the thoughts that fill it at other times, then the Spirit of God takes full and complete possession, and causes to pass before it the ideas or the images of thought that constitute the divine revelation to be made. Remember the tabernacle example?

2 Peter 1:21 says, "For no prophecy ever came by the will of man; but men spake from God, being moved by the Holy Spirit." Our consciousness and the certainty of a prophet's inner man being developed is clearly all about the manifestation of the Spirit of God within them. This does not happen if the soul is not in order. Let us now start to develop ourselves to experience growth as Issachar Seers. How does my soul prosper and what do we need to do? Keep reading.

CHAPTER 3

AWAKING THE SPIRITUAL SENSES

The Issachar seer was an interpreter and clarifier of eternal truth. Every seer, whether an Issachar Seer or not, has an enemy that hates the seer anointing and seeks to keep seers from stepping into the supernatural realm. The enemy knows that when the seer does begin to see and hear into the spirit realm, they will be empowered to manifest the Kingdom of Heaven in our sphere of influence.

This enemy of our very soul wants to hamper us from having a relationship with God. The enemy diligently works to make us spiritually blind and deaf. This is the bottom level of damage that he wants to do. Do not forget; you were created in God's very image to have a supernatural spiritual sense to see. You are a seer. This is the essence of the seer anointing.

So now before we go any further, do this. Take a deep breath and place your hand on your chest and say: "I am a seer. I am created in God's very image. I am supposed to see into God's plan, and I am supposed to see into God's spiritual Kingdom. This privilege is my spiritual inheritance through the finished work of Christ on the Cross." Do this at least three times a day. This is a prayer of faith and resilience, for you and me to encourage and strengthen our mind. The mind now processes this as our senses become alert.

Hebrews 5:14 says, "But strong meat belongeth to them that are of full age, even those who by reason of use have their senses exercised to discern both good and evil." Let us look at this to get a revelation concerning our spiritual senses. We know that there are five spiritual senses because they mirror the five natural senses of sight, hearing, tasting, smelling, and touching in the Spirit.

The Seer has five spiritual senses, but most of us choose to live by our physical senses. The reality is that if you develop as an Issachar Seer, you will not be able to rest solely on your physical senses. There is no way that the Issachar Prophet/Seer rested only the physical senses. Biblical times were difficult for those who lived then even though we believe our difficult times are now. The anti-Christ spirit now clearly has raised up to influence and work his wickedness in every facet of life.

There is not a lot of thought on the subject that we need direct contact with heaven. What is the Spirit teaching us? Clearly, we must as Seers/Prophets share and speak. Our souls (minds, will, emotions) must be renewed to the truth that God is answering and speaking in visions, heavenly encounters and even translations into other places normal Christianity may never go. How does this connect? How does this happen?

This is where we begin with the 'Process of Senses Enlightenment.' We must control the physical/flesh of our lives with the spiritual. The process of fasting is the key to allow us to do that. When we fast, we cover the mouth. We choose to also abstain from specific activities such as abstaining from food. Our food, for our physical body, sustains it and nourishes it.

God designed our bodies to be nourished and fueled, and yet there must be the nourishment of our Spirit. Matthew 4:4 (NIV) says, "It is written: 'Man does not live on bread alone, but on every word that comes from the mouth of God." Our soul needs this nourishment to fully connect with God.

The Issachar Seer knew that God's Word was as food that nourishes our spiritual life in the same way that physical food nourishes our physical life. When we eat our food, it strengthens and maintains our bodies. The Word of God nourishes, fuels, and strengthens our spirits. This is the key connection! Do you really want to develop as an Issachar Seer? The process starts with this understanding.

The prospective Issachar prophet needs to fast. There must be a letting go of the physical world. This includes your physical senses, and that is why you must fast. When we determine a set period, we focus now on our physical cravings versus our spiritual cravings.

This is not easy, and many times can be boring unless, again, we are dealing with the entire soul. The mind must be in a proper perspective. Can you imagine your spiritual hunger becoming stronger than your physical hunger? This is reflective of the Issachar prophet of the biblical days, as this prophet was extremely focused and not concerned about anything other than what God is saying and doing. The Issachar prophet had a will that was conditioned to achieve and demonstrate the true essence of focus.

You feed your spirit with the same enthusiasm as you do your body. Does your spiritual hunger take priority over physical hunger? Where is your soul on this issue? Prophet, you must be mature enough to understand that fasting is not a way to influence, impress, or manipulate God.

This is such a key fact because most prophets will tell you how many days they have fasted or how many years they have fasted and this reality proves nothing to God. This is so important because this act of impressing or bragging, and not in the will of God's plan.

Hebrews 4:13 (NIV) says, "Nothing in all creation is hidden from God's sight. Everything is uncovered and laid bare before the eyes of Him to whom we must give account." God knows us better than we know ourselves. In 2 Chronicles 20, we read the account of a fast King Jehoshaphat called for this very reason.

He had received a report that his enemies were allied against him and were nearly at his borders, and intent on making war against Israel. 2 Chronicles 20:1-2 (NIV) says, "After this, the Moabites and Ammonites with some of the Meunites came to make war on Jehoshaphat. Some men came and told Jehoshaphat: 'A vast army is coming against you from Edom, from the other side of the Dead Sea.'"

The report to Jehoshaphat was an accurate description of the situation as it appeared from those who spoke. This was key. Jehoshaphat was not willing to limit himself to what Tom, Dick, and Harry had to say. As a king and a leader, he trusted God. The soul of this leader was so in tune because there was a different type of relationship seen with God during Jehoshaphat's time.

Seers, even in your life, what situation confronts you today? Do the facts of your situation overwhelm you and cause you fear and anxiety? Do your circumstances look hopeless to you? The Spirit will never show you the point of view heaven has on your situation unless your soul is prospered by submitting to the Spirit.

The focus of the Issachar development is echoed as Jesus expected His disciples to fast. Matthew 6:16-18 (NIV) says, "When you fast, do not look somber as the hypocrites do, for they disfigure their faces to show men they are fasting. I tell you the truth; they have received their reward in full. "But when you fast, put oil on your head and wash your face, so that it will not be obvious to men that you are fasting, but only to your Father, who is unseen; and your Father, who sees what is done in secret, will reward you."

We see that Jesus often fasted as part of His ongoing life of prayer. Seers and Prophets whose lives have displayed the power and provision of God have made fasting part of their spiritual arsenal. This is a reflection on the Issachar gift. The focus and the display of knowledge of God's plan was the strength of their mantle. They were depended on by multiple areas of society. This was the backbone of needed wisdom given to leaders of that day.

In general, Prophets, let us be advised that the gift of discernment enables leaders empowered by God and people to determine the source of your voice as you utter what thus says the Lord. We discern the things of the Spirit through our basic five senses, which is the ability to hear, see, smell, touch, and taste.

As Prophets and Seers, The Lord will often "anoint" these natural areas to communicate something of the Spirit to us as follows. This was the case of the Issachar prophet who walked in such an anointing that was pointed and accurate as the natural senses of this prophet were able to be submitted to the communication with and of the Spirit of God at a constant supernatural level.

Now that we understand that our senses must rule on our spiritual side, I will share a defined separation of the soul and the spirit as we look at the blindness of the Prophet's soul in the next chapter. This will be necessary as we learn how to see things from our soul's perspective.

CHAPTER 4

DEALING WITH THE BLINDNESS OF THE PROPHET'S SOUL

One thing is sure there is a lot of word on miracles and blindness. There have been many miracles connected to blindness. Consider this thought it is no secret that being blind is especially crippling and looked upon as a deterrent to the ministry and the life of a prophet, especially in this day and time.

Looking beyond that level of blindness is another blind area to explore. The blindness of the prophet's soul is beyond the issue of loss of physical sight because we all know that a prophet's eyes can be open, and they may still not see.

The reality of Jesus going to the cross was for the healing of man's and the prophet's soul. The prophet cannot do the Kingdom work that has been assigned to him or her and be on the 'Prophetic Block.' That is a nice way of saying that you don't have any revelation, because your soul is blinded to the plans and work of God. You cannot walk in the Issachar gifting being blind in your soul. Prophet, when you are on a prophetic block and it is not fun.

The great Apostle Paul, shared with us in Ephesians 1:18-19 that "the eyes of your understanding being enlightened; that ye may know what is the hope of his calling, and what the riches of the glory of his inheritance in the saints, And what is the exceeding greatness of his power to us-ward who believe, according to the working of His mighty power."

Paul here is talking about being blind on the inside. He is speaking of the soul, the hope of his calling or what you were created to be, and that is a prophet. The riches of God's awesome glory of His inheritance is your prophetic gift. It is within you. Those prophets who will believe will operate in the unlimited power of the anointing. Understanding the issue is on the inside of you, not the outside. Your soul represents you. Now you're armed with information that will allow you to grow in your quest to operate in the Issachar gift.

This is why the prophet must be so careful because you will become a judge, jury and the hangman. Also as you can see things in other people and yet you do not see or cannot see these things in yourself. Therefore, the prophet so many times is blind, not on the outside, but you're blind on the inside. Prophet, it is what is on the inside of you that is killing you. The prophet's in-look determines the prophet's outlook.

Let us now demonstrate this. Look in Mark 8: 22-26.

22 And he cometh to Bethsaida; and they brought a blind man unto him and besought him to touch him. 23 And he took the blind man by the hand and led him out of the town; and when he had spit on his eyes, and put his hands upon him, he asked him if he saw ought.

24 And he looked up, and said, I see men as trees, walking. 25 After that he put his hands again upon his eyes and made him look up: and he was restored and saw every man clearly. 26 And he sent him away to his house, saying, neither go into the town, nor tell it to any in the town.

This story lets us know that healing is a progressive function. Bethsaida is a fishing port, a rough area and now Jesus has shown up. Notice the first thing Jesus does is lead the man out of his previous location. He leads him out of Bethsaida. He could have healed him in Bethsaida, but the reality is until the blind man could see his community differently, his outlook will not change. Until you, the prophet of God, can see from your soul, your outlook will never change.

You will always see the issues of others and not yourself. Your soul will be blind and your relationship with God will suffer because you are not able to see the entire picture, scene, and vision that God is showing you.

Prophets, we must consider that this man's condition is being fed by his environment, like many of us. We are locked in a place mentally, we never understand our purpose or destiny simply because we are preconditioned by a custom, trait, saying, or even a norm of our environment.

Just for historical reference, Bethsaida was a cursed city, and because it had a history of unbelief in God and striving to be dysfunctional. Notice that Jesus spit on the man. His spit is more anointed, more precious than all the treasure of Bethsaida. Can you imagine Jesus spitting on you?

The man did not get angry. He simply wanted to get out of his situation. He realized he had an issue. How many prophets have we seen around the world, who have issues, real deep personal issues and will act like they have nothing wrong with them, and it's everybody else's fault? The spit of Jesus may not be so dignified for some of us.

Maybe we should consider that to not be offended is a luxury of those who do not hold onto issues, which prevent them from moving forward. This blind man was ready to see. He was humble and hungry enough. He was ready for whatever the healer had for him.

He could not afford to be insulted. He needed the miracle more than he needed to be insulted about Jesus spitting on his eyes. How many of us could handle that? Consider how the anointing will humble us to a point where it is all that matters.

Look at us. We will tell God what we do not want to do, where we do not want to go, and who we do not want to connect with all because we think we are in control of the narrative. The reality is that we are so blind to the real issues, we miss the blessing because our soul has been cut off from the Spirit of God, and we are going through the motions.

The reality today is we, the prophet, are not hungry enough for God. Let's consider that our current level of trouble has not elevated us enough to the point where nothing else matters, and all we want is God worse than we want our next breath. That is when you get to the point of a new reality, looking and seeing outside of your environment.

Where are the prophets of God who are desperate for the anointing? Desperation is a tool that will drive the prophet to the presence of God in a powerful way. You will stop making excuses when you're desperate. You will stop blaming issues on your heritage, environment, other prophets, other apostles, and your goals. Your focus will be to get out of the situation. Again, where are the desperate prophets/seers who want to see change, miracles, signs, and wonders?

The blind man's emotions, will, and mind were focused on the right perspective. Imagine Jesus spitting on him and asking the man what he sees. The man says he sees men who walk as trees. Notice that your outlook is always a reflection of what is in you.

He sees what was on his mind. He has, for his entire life, heard people, imagined how they looked and now reflects on his perspective of men. As prophets, our process of looking at people will always reflect who we are and what we come from until we fully submit to God and allow our souls to engage in spiritual prosperity.

The blind man is better, but he is not whole. This is the first stage of recovery for his life. The reality is that Jesus knew his situation. He needed more of the life-changing anointing upon his life.

How many of us prophets need more of the anointing? We know we need it, and will still act as we have arrived. We are ready to mentor the whole world, but we have been nowhere and done nothing. We are ready to judge our peers and teach them ways we know absolutely nothing about.

We are settling for less, prophets. Have you ever heard the saying, "I am not what I want to be, but I am better than I was." Really? Why are you settling for less when more is available? We serve a God of more than enough, overflow, abundance, and yet why is the prophet of today willing to settle for less, so that we can run around and say we are a prophet/Seer and impress people? This blind man needed more, and he knew it.

He, like the prophets, still does not see people clearly. You're anointed but your outlook is negative. You're anointed but you're lazy. You are anointed but you are a procrastinator. You are anointed, but you're a gossiper. You're anointed but you're easily intimidated. Prophet, what do you want?

Do you want to see partially, or do you want to really see through the motives, shames, schemes, and plots of men? Do you really want to look in the future and see what God is getting ready to do? Those of you who want to see on this level need to understand you must be whole. Your soul must not be blinded. You must see beyond the surface and see into the deep.

When we do not have the proper outlook, as prophets, we contaminate everyone we meet. Where did you come from? Yes, you will see some of your peers who will not need what you need. They will not require what you require. The point is we saw many healed for the first time. They had a touch from God, but let us consider where this man came from: environment, background, and surrounding company. The reality is that he is not you. What he needed, you may not need from God. You may already have it.

Different prophets will have different needs from God, and yes, some will need more in certain areas than others. Every prophet is different, just like every man is different. So we must look at ourselves and not become judge and jury on what your prophetic peer may need. The reality is we must individually get our souls off prophetic block.

Why will you need to keep getting a touch from God? This man needed another touch from God. The issue is whatever it takes for you to see like Jesus, and to be functional in the fullness of your calling-you must get. Are you willing to seek God again?

Jesus laid hands on him, and now he could see as Jesus saw. Whatever it takes. When Elijah was translated into heaven, he told Elisha, "If you can see me, you can have what I have and have it double." The key is you and I as prophets must-see.

So, when we are released, healed, and able to see through the eyes of our understanding, and we are off the prophetic block. Remember, our goals and ambition shift because of our vision shifts. We, the prophets, would be wise to take on Philippians 3:13-14 and adapt it for our new sight in Christ.

Say it out loud as you read it." Brethren, I count not myself to have apprehended: but this one thing I do, forgetting those things which are behind, and reaching forth unto those things which are before. I press toward the mark for the prize of the high calling of God in Christ Jesus."

Even the prophet Samuel found himself thrust in a situation where his mentor, Eli, was on prophetic block. Samuel was granted the ability to see and communicate with God in a whole new way. Eli was not.

His life changed, and he never went back. You would be wise, Prophet, to do the same. Look at someone and say, "I am not going back to the place that I once was in. My soul is clear, and I see clearly what God is showing me." This is how we start to deal with the strongholds that we all have.

CHAPTER 5

THE STRONGHOLDS OF A SEER'S SOUL

Satan's goal is clear and direct. He has tasked himself and his demonic army to keep the Seers of God in a state of preputial darkness. Satan cannot deal directly with the Spirit of God, but he can and will deceive God's elect, such as you, the Seers of God. The place this happens is in the Seer's soul with strongholds that give us false and misleading information about God.

The demonic ability to distort our knowledge of God fosters erroneous and inadequate ways, habits, and norms of our life. There is no doubt many seers are emotionally weakened and held in spiritual bondage. 2 John 3 says that if we are going to prosper, then it will be our soul that becomes the first recipient so that every other area of our life prospers.

This was the Issachar Seer, and yet they were almost always in support of a leader or movement. The Issachar Seer will challenge beliefs, customs, and traditions with the Word of God. Two key and important scriptures are 2 Timothy 2:15 and John 8:31-32.

John 8:31-32 (NIV) says, "To the Jews who had believed him," and, "If you hold to my teaching, you are really my disciples. Then you will know the truth, and the truth will set you free."

2 Timothy 2:15 says, "Study to shew thyself approved unto God, a workman that needed not to be ashamed, rightly dividing the word of truth." The Scripture says we need not be ashamed, but have you wondered how we made God ashamed by not adhering to His Word because of the strongholds of a seer's soul? Is this because of our inability to study and gain knowledge from His Word? God's Word in the life of a Seer is critical as we look at the soul of the seer.

For the seer, we need to establish and understand that strongholds exist and have the power to withhold you from reaching your destiny. This is an ongoing battle between good and evil in the life of every seer. Every seer must decide one way or another that you will become relevant, and choose to equip yourself to be able to move forward in your calling of God.

The toughest battles of a seer's life are to endure are the spiritual battles that the strongholds will manifest in your soul. Consider the things that can weigh you down from reaching the heights the Lord has for you. Seers deal with the strongholds of hopelessness and helplessness. The same strongholds and others can nullify a seers' will. This will make you reject your visions, dreams and then condemn yourself as the world condemns you for what they do not understand about you. Make no mistake that seers are going to deal with the common symptoms of strongholds like low self-esteem, a guilty conscience, feeling worthless, and condemnation. Other seers will deal with shameful thinking and erratic behavior among the array of negative thoughts and stale desires that are available in this world to hold you in check.

The issues of a strong family, customs and traditions that have held you back to the point where you have not been able to achieve in your past are now in your present. Seers and prophets do not be fooled. Strongholds exist within your soul and have the power to withhold you from reaching your destiny.

To expand on this topic, customs and traditions are a deeper layer of strongholds. We first need to deal with the thoughts, the norms and the idea of the spirit and the soul being as one in an individual person. Let's first look at Hebrews 4:12 which says, "For the word of God is quick, and powerful, and sharper than any two-edged sword, piercing even to the dividing asunder of Soul and spirit, and of the joints and marrow, and is a discerner of the thoughts and intents of the heart."

Every seer needs to understand that the Word of God separates spiritual things that seem completely intertwined, such as the soul and spirit. The Word of God can and will distinguish between the godly and ungodly that the life of a seer will attract.

The soul and spirit seem indistinguishable; most of us throughout our lives have brought into this idea. This incredible "cutting" power of Scripture is a tool to separate our very thoughts into good and evil.

John 6:63 says, "It is the spirit that quickeneth; the flesh profiteth nothing: the words that I speak unto you, they are spirit, and they are life." Ephesians 1:3 says, "Blessed be the God and Father of our Lord Jesus Christ, who hath blessed us with all spiritual blessings in heavenly places in Christ." The spirit is perfected, but we see that the soul of a seer is a constant process of development.

We see that our soul identifies with our bodies. Psalms 139:14 says, "I will praise thee; for I am fearfully and wonderfully made: marvelous are thy works; and that my Soul knoweth right well." 3 John 2 says, "Beloved, I wish above all things that thou mayest prosper and be in health, even as thy Soul prospereth." Let us clearly see that your soul is not your spirit. This is a fatal flaw with many of our spiritual upbringings.

We have not addressed the issues of our soul because we felt it was a spirit issue. The Word tells us that the spirit is made perfected or quickened and the flesh does not prosper. The strongholds of our souls have maintained their place in our lives.

Every seer needs to seek the wisdom of a healthy soul. This is the process of learning how to correct the problems of his or her soul caused by strongholds. The seer must learn this as the promised prosperity of God comes through the soul. Do we know what part of our life we want to prosper in?

Can you examine your soul? Seer/Prophet, what has not prospered in your life because of a stronghold that is residing and believes it has the total right to be there? Romans 12:2 is where the work of the soul starts.

The work of the mind is the master element of your soul. Another part of the soul is identified in Romans 9:1 which says, "I say the truth in Christ, I lie not, my conscience also bearing me witness in the Holy Ghost." We are talking about the emotions here.

Philippians 2:13 says, "For it is God which worketh in you both to will and to do of his good pleasure." The will of God is at work in your life. Now, we see in Scripture the identity of the soul and God's plans for our souls.

As Seers of God, we look at our souls and see the partnership we have with God. We should ponder now how to eliminate our strongholds. We want the promised prosperity, wealth, health, and blessings of God upon our lives.

Because we want what God has for us, we must learn the work of 1 John 2:27 which says, "But the anointing which ye have received of him abideth in you, and ye need not that any man teach you: but as the same anointing teacheth you of all things, and is truth, and is no lie, and even as it hath taught you, ye shall abide in him."

We should realize that if the spirit is to be perfected in us, then we must realize that our soul needs work. The Spirit of God teaches our spirits. Then our spirits teach our soul. Say Bingo! The issue is our souls will not receive because of our personal strongholds.

2 Corinthians 10: 4-5 says, "(For the weapons of our warfare are not carnal, but mighty through God to the pulling down of strong holds;) Casting down imaginations, and every high thing that exalteth itself against the knowledge of God, and bringing into captivity every thought to the obedience of Christ."

This is talking about your soul. Your spirit is perfected and there is no stronghold there. The strongholds are in our soul. This is our hold up to prosperity and destiny. The mere fact that God will give us what we have asked even though our souls are in disarray is mind-boggling. This is key in developing an Issachar Seer.

Genesis 11:6 says, "And the Lord said, Behold, the people is one, and they have all one language; and this they begin to do: and now nothing will be restrained from them, which they have imagined doing." The imagination of Seers and Prophets has always been a sore spot in the development of the prophetic gift. Many times, our imagination can and will serve as our greatest enemy. We are thinking things should be a certain way and that way may not be in the will of God. So now our imagination is an enemy to us and serves as a detour from our destiny.

Now let us imagine the total opposite. Imagine now again if you are on one accord with God, you will be able to imagine a blessing and you will be able to receive it. Now consider Psalms 37:4, which says, "Delight thyself also in the Lord: and he shall give thee the desires of thine heart." When your soul is placed in the right perspective with God, then you shall see a level of prosperity that we do not see in the body of Christ.

This is critical for a seer, as many of us have seen over and over that the prophetic anointing is a magnet for prosperity. This is a special partnership that God wants for His seers and prophets. The reality is that in the faith partnership that the seer has with God, our souls must be trained and mentored.

While most of us have been raised up believing that the spirit and the soul are the same, we can and should clearly see that they are different in which one is perfected in the anointing of God and the other is a work in progress of receiving that perfecting. Why is this important? Let us look at the church of today, and the body of Christ today. It starts with Hosea 4:6.

Hosea 4:6 says, "My people are destroyed for lack of knowledge: because thou hast rejected knowledge, I will also reject thee, that thou shalt be no priest to me: seeing thou hast forgotten the law of thy God, I will also forget thy children."

This is the Word of God that blankets the church today, and the entire Body of Christ. We can argue, debate and spiritually reason on this, but it still says what it says. We are passing down generational ignorance, especially in prosperity, and other areas of our life because we have a lack of knowledge.

Case in point, have you ever really examined why the body of Christ and many churches today frown on prosperity? Prosperity is not popular in the church because of a lack of knowledge on the topic. We have allowed people's thoughts and perceptions to become strongholds. We have a lack of knowledge today on the issues of our blessings, especially prosperity.

Isaiah 5:13 says, "Therefore my people are gone into captivity, because they have no knowledge: and their honorable men are famished, and their multitude dried up with thirst. This is an issue of the Soul, with the mind to begin with being caught up in captivity."

This tells every seer and prophet that we must get the knowledge to empower our children's children. This means we must get some training. Training in this generation is critical. We need to be able to expand and develop this anointing.

CHAPTER 6

SEEKING AND TRAINING FOR THE ISSACHAR ANOINTING

The Issachar Anointing was given to a unique group of people that always knew the timing and plan of God. The Issachar gift was a gift of perception and wisdom. The ability to operate in such discernment, that understanding of the times, and the seasons, makes them essential to Israel and all that they served. The gift of understanding is always a great benefit to all to whom it is assigned to serve.

The Issachar Anointing today is the unique anointing of seers that will enable them to also understand the times and seasons. They are able to influence and lead nations in such a time as we live in now. The aspect of the gift that is so important is that as a prophet, you can use the Issachar anointing to understand the times /seasons that govern your life and then leverage the Issachar anointing to change the times/seasons to favor you.

The Issachar gift was birthed by God in a period when Israel needed leadership. This gift clearly discerned the moves of God. The flow of this type of knowledge was critical for God appointed leaders to listen to and for nations to abide by.

Let's look at Jacob's blessing of Issachar in Genesis 49:14-15. Issachar was described as a strong donkey, lying down between two burdens. He saw that the rest was good and that the land was pleasant. Issachar, who was known as a personal individual, bowed his shoulder to bear a burden and became a band of slaves.

Let us get real. This really does not sound like a blessing. The prophetic utterance was meant to match the personality of Issachar. Issachar was a different kind of leader. He is like today's Issachar prophets, who are different types of prophets. Some may say they are wild and strong-willed, but still operate under a strong level of discipline. The reality is these attributes are significant needed attributes to function and survive in the world today.

This is the type of prophet called to bear the burden of gossip, slander, and even rejection. This type of prophet will face a significant amount of rejection because of the closeness and accuracy of discernment of knowing God's plan and understanding of the seasons/times.

The mantle of understanding is the gift of the Issachar anointed prophet. The ability of each prophet to develop information, process it to become a revelation, so they not only see the condition, but they can also understand what God wants said through this condition.

This is priceless because regardless of what is before them, Issachar's prophets are never afraid of the storms of life. Understand fear may be there, but they are not afraid. The Issachar prophet is prepared for and to get through the storms because of their unique understanding.

The same gift is available today as we call on the Issachar anointed prophets to move forth and inform us of the times and seasons of this generation. We should also consider that the Issachar gift can be connected to a Watchman or an Apostle. The gift is a multidimensional gift for a seer to accomplish missions and assignments.

Those, today who seek this gift at a high level should be aware of the rigorous regiment that they will need to follow, master and mature in, for the gift of Issachar to flourish within the mantle that is upon their life. The length will vary from seer to seer.

While every seer matures in their body, their mind or soul (mind, will, emotions, intellect, imagination) and they also mature spiritually. This is done by exercising their spiritual senses. The five spiritual senses are the same as the five natural senses of sight, hearing, tasting, smelling, and touching in the spirit.

Seers have five spiritual senses, but most are living by their five physical senses. We, the Issachar prophets, are moving with the spiritual senses and expressing through the five physical senses. The prophets who understand that these are the most difficult times mankind has ever experienced will fight to break through the reality of moving in the spiritual senses.

This is where the Issachar anointed prophets do their work. Our work base as Issachar prophets is to share, instruct and guide those whom they are assigned. Additionally, Issachar prophet's demonstrate accuracy and maturity that only comes through a command of our physical senses as they submit to our spiritual senses.

There is a sureness on the part of the Issachar prophet to know what is always going on around us by the Spirit. This requires our spiritual senses to be enlightened. Our need for God to guide, speak and show us things to come is constant. Any candidate for the Issachar anointing must renew your mind to the truth that angels, visions, heavenly encounters and even translations into other places is a normal spiritual activity in the supernatural lifestyle of an Issachar Prophet.

There are several personal attributes that must be mastered for this gift to function as one with any seer. Let's look at these traits and understand why they are vital to the development of an Issachar anointed prophet, watchman, or apostle.

1. The Issachar Seer's Mentality

The mentality of the Issachar anointing is that your sufficiency is derived totally from God. This was true of all Issachar anointed seers. The Issachar Seers were a group of prophets who recognized that their sufficiency is of God. There was an awesome Sovereign blessing among and in their lives.

There is a formula that is followed. The Issachar seer is willing to submit themselves willingly and peacefully to their leadership and do the will of God. Wow! What a novel idea. God loves the unity among the anointed of this gift. Psalms 133:1-4 says, "Behold, how good and how pleasant it is for brethren to dwell together in unity! It is like the precious ointment upon the head, that ran down upon the beard, even Aaron's beard: that went down to the skirts of his garments; 3 As the dew of Hermon, and as the dew that descended upon the mountains of Zion: for there the Lord commanded the blessing, even life forevermore."

2. The faith of an Issachar Seer was a clinic in the fight of faith.

The Issachar anointed seers were a group of people who knew what it was to fight the good fight of faith. For a seer to fight the good fight of faith means that the seer must abide in the word by faith, no matter or regardless of what the seer may feel. This can be extremely uncomfortable to develop, but it is worth it. This understanding of the fight of faith is priceless because regardless of what is before them, Issachar prophets are never afraid of the storms of life. The Issachar prophet is prepared for the storm and beyond the storms. This includes what we may or may not understand. Matthew 16:24 says, "Then said Jesus unto his disciples, if any man will come after me, let him deny himself, and take up his cross, and follow me."

3. The Issachar seer understands the need for change.

Many prophets/seers by their situation are in a type of training to develop the Issachar gift upon their lives. This type of prophet finds themselves in a place of change, and they know they need to change but they do not see or understand how change will manifest itself. The biblical Issachar prophet was always in a situation where he or she knew the change was necessary.

The Issachar prophet is known to trust God at an unnatural level, and they did not worry about it because they knew that the Lord was involved in all endeavors concerning them. They also know that whatever God is going to do, it is suddenly within his timing. This is the peace of the Issachar prophet. The peace within their soul. Change needs to happen and they were aware of the change and were all too grateful to be a part of change, but they did not have to be the face of the change. They were more than often the skeletal background. They were the backbone of leadership.

Today, this type of anointing is needed as God will select His chosen to be the face of a situation, but He will position others for the support of the situation. This is the unity that we see demonstrated within the gift. This is also what we see today. Many times, when groups of prophets and seers never learn how to work with each other, because everyone feels they are supposed to be upfront or the face of a situation.

Clearly, we see God developed this gifting at the highest levels within a group of seers working in unison. Look at Deborah's life as they worked together to back and elevate her as a judge and as a prophet. Today's prophets who have trouble working with their peers will also have problems developing the Issachar gifting.

This anointing connects to your life for special seasons of training and empowerment. Today for a prophet to know they are in God's timing and God's hand is upon you is priceless. Isaiah 41:10 (NIV) says, "Fear not, for I am with you; be not dismayed, for I am your God; I will strengthen you, I will help you, I will uphold you with my righteous right hand."

Judges 5:15 (NIV) says, " And the princes of Issachar were with Deborah; As was Issachar, so was Barak; Into the valley they rushed at his heels..." A prophet that is under the Issachar anointing is released to move into wisdom within any situation that he or she may encounter. Can God trust you with this type of anointing?

Your dependence upon God is so critical in this aspect that the wisdom and insight of an Issachar prophet is of the supernatural. The Issachar anointing is an apostolic anointing, of knowing what is coming, and to know how to implement divine strategies and plans to accomplish the will of God. The Issachar gift was critical for the past times and it is still crucial in this hour and time.

What does the Issachar anointing do in the life of a seer? There are several things, but every seer is unique and different. I want to point out some general traits that need to be developed for you to operate in various seasons.

1. Understand that your life has been set up by God. He is the master life conductor. Despite our thoughts of what we may think or feel, God is in charge period.

2. There will be seasons in your development of the Issachar gift of disappointment, emotional breaking, and seasons of unnatural favor, as you move through life. The fact is you must be thankful for every season and time and learn how to recognize them.

3. Your identity and character will develop as you will see change. You will learn how to embrace it and know that you're moving at the right time and place. Destiny is within your reach if you follow God. This

is your total surrender, your total dependence upon God, regardless of the situation.

4. Remember this point and do not ever forget it. You must understand that your life experiences have and will prepare you for the placement as an Issachar gift to the body of Christ. Your emotions and will are as one with the plan of God.

5. The Issachar anointing gives you a thirst for more of God. We see Issachar anointed prophets with a thirst for more knowledge of God. They hunt for revelation and understand that when you are anointed by an Issachar anointing, you will see that your voice and ideas can change or influence the major structure in all the areas of your life.

6. Once we receive the Issachar Anointing, we can become influential, that's why maturity must be a vital part of this gift. We must understand that our voice will be heard by those who may not be familiar with us, as God exposes us to other influential leaders and officials and situations, we may or may not have been mentored in.

So, if you struggle to understand how to become an Issachar prophet, understand you must build up your spiritual immune system for Kingdom business. The development of Prophetic discernment is critical.

Prophetic discernment is not developed because you go to a church, or even go to a prophetic meeting. Prophetic discernment is developed only with a relationship with God. The Issachar prophet is not lazy, and this prophet understands the moment he or she is in.

The 'Issachar Anointing Prophet' is ready to do the same thing over and over, like pray (over and over), fast (over and over) until the breakthrough comes forth. Once this is done in the spiritual realm, the prophet communicates in the accuracy of their utterance. The theme of training in the life of an Issachar Seer can and will take many roles. One role every prophet must deal with is the role of understanding the mentality of being a prophet. Now we need to discuss the Eschatology of the soul of a prophet. This will be critical in the art of constant training and development.

CHAPTER 7

THE ESCHATOLOGY OF A PROPHET'S TORMENTED SOUL

In previous chapters, we have covered that the soul is made up of the mind, will, and emotions of a person. Whether you're a prophet or not, this is a fact for everyone. The reality of prophets being tested is not new; but for many prophets, there seems to be no real end to the issues of life.

There is a saying we use so much in life and the Body of Christ, "If it ain't one thing, then no doubt it is another." While it is not my assignment to debate the merit of that statement, there must be an ending, a sign of competition, the end of a season, or an age. This is the Eschatology of a prophet's tormented soul, the ending of the torment, and the ending of waging war with the same enemy over and over. Eschatology is the science of the last things.

As a prophet of God, called and assigned by God, there are things in all of our lives we want to see end. Things that have tested us, frustrated us, and have simply affected the effectiveness of the gift we present to the Body of Christ today.

As we mature in the prophetic, we start to realize that until some things in our life end, we will never see a new season of prosperity, and we will always think and reason in a defeated fashion. God will never be glorified in the manner we should demonstrate in our lives, and we are simply stuck in the moment of recurring time. We are not living one moment of life after the other. We are stuck because we cannot pass the test before us.

The prophet Isaiah Israel was challenged by the experience with the Babylonians. Imagine the prophet, with the gift of being a long-distance seer, an eagle eye prophet who is seeing Israel, a country that has been ripped totally away from their culture for years. Now that God has brought them out of the bondage, there is still a problem. Mentally, they are still in the bondage.

Isaiah 43:18-19 says, "Remember ye, not the former things, neither consider the things of old. Behold, I will do a new thing; now it shall spring forth; shall ye not know it? I will even make a way in the wilderness and rivers in the desert." While it is true, you will never forget some things that have happened. You cannot waddle in it and make it your life's work. Stop complaining about the past that you can't change or undo.

So please understand that the people here are tormented not so much as by the experience but more by the memory. How many prophets do you know who may be in the same situation? God brought you out of the situation, but you are tormented by the mere mention of it, even repeatedly.

Some prophets are tormented by memory. Some may be tormented in their dream life, relationships, physical disorders, and the mere mention of their life's indignity. This was real for the people, and today it is real for some within the prophetic family of seers to include prophets, watchmen, prophetesses, and yes, even the apostles.

Torment and the sting will never seem to go away. Have you ever had someone you may know well come up to you and say, "I remember you when you_____?" These people do not always mean harm, but the way they communicate the issue brings up those old depressing memories that dominate your life.

This has been described within the community of prophets as the ministry of torment. The ministry of torment is not just limited to prophets, but it is effective in the goal of keeping God's chosen prophets in bondage long after the experience is over. Therefore, the eschatology of a prophet's tormented soul is needed.

There are prophets who do not trust anyone because they got backstabbed twenty years ago. The thought here is to not be careful but learn how to deal with the issues, so the issues do not camouflage your anointing. The prophet must learn how to curse the spirit of intimidation and arrest the ministry of torment or you will be forever taking this same test and not passing it.

Test yourself, prophet. Do the same issues, same enemy, or same devil torment you? Are you faced with the same incidents over and over? Yes, even when you accept a new challenge, you see the same issues. Are the issues of your 20's and 30's the same with you in your 40's, 50's, 60's? Are you clear on who told you it was okay to be tormented and just accept it as your issue of life?

God hates your old enemies. Look at a Psalm of David. David says in Psalm 5:1-7, "Give ear to my words, O Lord, consider my meditation. Hearken unto the voice of my cry, my king, and my God: for unto thee will I pray. My voice shalt thou hear in the morning, O Lord; in the morning will I direct my prayer unto thee and will look up. For thou art not a God that hath pleasure in wickedness: neither shall evil dwell with thee. The foolish shall not stand in thy sight: thou hatest all workers of iniquity. Thou shalt destroy them that speak leasing: The Lord will abhor the bloody and deceitful man. But as for me, I will come into thy house in the multitude of thy mercy: and in thy fear will I worship toward thy holy temple."

David is clear on how God feels about an enemy. To bring this thought in a clearer context: there was an enemy that God hated greatly. This was an enemy of God and the people of God. This enemy tormented God's people over and over. I am talking about the Amalekites. 1 Samuel 15:3 says, "Go and attack Amalek," Samuel tells Saul, speaking for God: "Utterly destroy all that they have; do not spare them, but kill both man and woman, child and infant, ox and sheep, camel and donkey."

In 1 Samuel 15:9, we see Saul carries out the command—though he preserves everything of economic value, along with the Amalekite king, Agag. "All that was despised and worthless, they utterly destroyed." Saul did it but did it his way. He did not kill and destroy everything.

Why did God almost instantly replace him in his Kingship? Just like the prophetic, is it different? The precedence that Saul set as Israel's first king would influence all his successors. The precedence we set as prophets of God influences the way people receive us and listen when we say, "Thus saith the Lord."

We can see how Saul messed up, as he was already on this ice with God for his foolish sacrifices. Yet we see God granted another chance granted for Saul. God commanded Saul to destroy the Amalekites, not to preserve their history.

Have you ever noticed that God told you precisely how to do something and you did it your way? You would have benefitted, but now you are still troubled, still tormented because you had a better way. Again, we see that just like the prophet of today. Saul's lack of focus, lack of attention to detail cost him greatly. What has your lack of focus and lack of detail cost you?

Let us, just for a minute, look at Saul as the prophet of today. How many times have we been given direct, clear instructions by God to do something a certain way and when we do it our way. On the surface, it looks good, but the reality is that it does not work.

When it does not work, you find yourself-tormented with your demons of record, who have been there with you throughout your life. Make no mistake: the soul is tormented, and it must end—matter of fact, my assignment with you is to alert you to this very fact.

Look at us. Are we or are we not still found with the same tormented spirit? For some of us, it is our granddaddy's demon, or grandmothers or even deeper in our generational lineage. There is no change. We are crying out to God for answers for direction. Has it ever seemed like God is not speaking to us? The lesson is hard when we forget that the teacher is always silent during the test.

Have you ever considered the reason why you are taking the same test over yet again? You want the test to end, but here again, God puts the test before you. He is silent, and waiting for you to pass the test. As you and I so often proclaim, we are waiting on God and the unspoken reality is that God is waiting for us to do what is needed.

Do you see what Saul did wrong, prophet? Saul was instructed to destroy all, to include everything and everyone. Saul did it his way. He collected things that looked good to him. That is not what God told him to do through the prophet. God's directive through the prophet Samuel was for him specifically to destroy all, to include the king.

A question to ponder: Why did God hate the Amalekites so much? There are stories of the scribes of that era who blotted their names out of writings to symbolize God's hatred for this group of people. We must look at the character of the Amalekites as they were simply the most vicious people ever. The Amalekites symbolized an old enemy.

They specialized in attacking their enemies in the enemy's weakest areas. The Amalekites used your weakness against you. They would rather attack your women and children than your warriors. This is who they were. They are treacherous, evil and have no conscience. This was an enemy who would simply always go after your weakness.

This is a characteristic of a tormented soul, as the spirit of the Amalekites attacks over and over in the soul of a seer and is set out to destroy the gift. Deuteronomy 25:11 says, "When men strive together one with another, and the wife of the one draweth near for to deliver her husband out of the hand of him that smiteth him, and putteth forth her hand, and taketh him by the secrets." Picture the Amalekites as the woman who punches the man in his secrets, with the word being translated as genitals.

2 Corinthians 12:9 says, "My grace is sufficient for you, for my power is made perfect in weakness." Therefore, I will boast more gladly of my weaknesses, so that the power of Christ may rest upon me." Weakness was never meant to be the enemy's weapon to cause sin and confusion, but for the Amalekites it was. Your weakness was always God's tool to build faith and reliance on Him.

Joshua fought the Amalekites in Rephidim as they attacked Israel. This is when Moses held up his prophetic staff in the warfare position. Joshua's battle with the Amalekites was a long battle and Moses grew tired. That is why Aaron and Hur were there to help hold up the arms of Moses.

The Amalekites represent an enemy in your life that is redundant and was committed to fighting you repeatedly. This enemy does not intend to give up. This is an old enemy, who many times, is generational to the prophet. I am talking about the spirit of the Amalekites.

Many prophets have fought their way through life and the reality is that some prophets have grown tired. Anyone will, especially if they must fight repeatedly? Think about the Amalekite type enemy of your life, who, what or where is it and why does it torment you repeatedly? Why does the mention of it do that? Prophet you have grown older and your personal enemy is still there in your soul. This enemy has grown with you.

To make matters worse, this enemy has long been defeated in your life and yet the question on the table is if the enemy is defeated, why is there still that enemy in your memory just as vivid as the day it was established as your enemy?

Look at Joshua's battle with them again in Rephidim. Finally, he defeated them. The issue is that he defeated the enemy, but he did not destroy the enemy. A defeated enemy can regroup and possibly come back. A destroyed enemy is just that. Look at what God said. Prophet, grab this concept.

Exodus 17:14-16 (NIV) says, "Then the Lord said to Moses, "Write this on a scroll as something to be remembered and make sure that Joshua hears it, because I will completely blot out the name of Amalek from under heaven." Moses built an altar and called it The Lord is my Banner. He said, "Because hands were lifted up against the throne of the Lord, the Lord will be at war against the Amalekites from generation to generation." Defeating an enemy will kill the tormenting enemy of the past and present. Killing that enemy will defeat the enemy forever.

Exodus 14:13 (NIV) says, "Moses told the people, "Don't be afraid. Just stand where you are and watch the Lord rescue you. The Egyptians that you see today will never be seen again." The Lord Himself will fight for you. You won't have to lift a finger in your defense!"

Can you adopt this for the torment of your soul? To the Seer Nation of Prophets, Prophetesses, Watchman and Apostles, simply put enough is clearly enough! Let every situation or circumstance be a lie as we allow God to be the truth in your life. Can you proclaim that in the mighty name of Jesus?

To those prophets who are dealing with arrogant ancestral, generational spirits, with Amalekite like tendencies who are monitoring and frustrating your life, speak to them now! Call out their unproductive stubborn spiritual spouses of shame and embarrassment everywhere you go. Call them out: the ill-mannered wicked witches and wizards scattering, stealing, killing, and destroying your life and on assignment to destroy your ministry. Speak to them now in the name of Jesus. Those enforcers of satanic laws that have been instituted against you are being consumed right now by the pure fire of the Holy Ghost, in the mighty name of Jesus! Oh, my God, gives us true words for the appropriate time.

CHAPTER 8

THE POWER OF THE ISSACHAR PROPHETS SPOKEN WORD

True words inspire trust and confidence; lies break trust, and doubt and suspicion replace confidence. The soul and the words it processes are central to our most meaningful relationships. An example would be that we confidently and readily do business with people whom we can affirm are ones who keep their word. People who do not do this dissolve the grounds for their own enduring success. The mind, will, and emotions are working in unison to produce desired results.

As prophets, let's note that it is perhaps among the most humbling attributes of God's ways. He humbles with His gift to benefit mankind. He confers upon us, His prophets a staggering degree of power. This is backed by a responsibility in the capacity of our words to cause things to happen. Words have power. Within the broad scope of this remarkable truth, the privilege and power of speaking blessings upon people came into view.

Let us consider the opening Words of the Bible; the power of the spoken word is its own evidence. Words are not only how creation was made, but also the substance and the stuff of which the creative realm is shaped. "And God said" appears in the Genesis text, and the next thing, what God said appears in our world.

The power of words is not evident just when God uses them in creating. It is also evident in His ways that teach us how to live within that creation. We are the creation. God's word and His laws are essentially God's guidelines for making life "work" in this realm.

The Issachar prophet was known for their words and obedience. People came to get the wisdom of their word as it always aligned with the force of His words. In contrast, when disobedience refuses God's word and laws, the opposite of blessing ensues.

The power of the spoken word of the Issachar seer can best be understood by the establishment of covenants with people such as leaders, businesspeople, and even community leaders of the day of the Issachar seer. That is the influence we should seek and the influence we can expect when our souls line up with God's perspective on a situation.

Thus, the Issachar prophet demonstrated the power of words, as seen in creation and our covenants. We look at the lives of other prophets of God, and we see how powerful a spoken word was just as if it was with an Issachar prophet. The power of spoken words can best be understood as we see the powerful Melchizedek, as he blesses Abraham. He blesses Abraham, who is God's first prophet. He applauds his protection, victory, and Abraham's tithing (Genesis 14:18-24).

What separated these prophets? What was in them that connected them to the anointing of action? We should look no further than the soul. Here is the one connection in the life of these prophets and the prophets of today. The soul is a key element. Let's examine the soul of these individuals.

Carefully look here as we are creatures who normally follow our convictions. We are going to do things that will always reflect our current mentality level. Abraham's actions were the actions of a mature prophet. He was not an ego swollen immature prophet. The reality of his world is he did not have the time or the will to be that. His emotions and feelings were shown here as great personal prophetic growth. This is an Issachar prophet, or in this case, Abraham, we see in command of his personal issues.

Samson offers us special insight into how the spoken word is so effective with these prophets' lives. Judges 14:5-7 says, "Then went Samson down, and his father and his mother, to Timnath, and came to the vineyards of Timnath: and behold, a young lion roared against him. And the Spirit of the Lord came mightily upon him, and he rent him as he would have rent a kid, and he had nothing in his hand: but he told not his father or his mother what he had done. And he went down, and talked with the woman, and she pleased Samson well."

There are questions to be answered of Samson, just like there are questions to be answered in our personal prophetic lives. Are you aware of what the enemy is doing to you right now? How are you dealing with the conflict you are feeling inside? Nowadays, most prophets will have an outside shield of everything being alright, but inside, they need a private breakthrough.

Most of us are living with things on the inside we are not settled with. We are like Samson, who has a conflict with his values, faith, and parents. Samson is living with challenges like most prophets. The life of the prophet must be filled with substance that matches the DNA of the prophetic profile of the prophet. Understand this, people who walk with you must be of the same Prophetic DNA as you or they are simply going for a stroll at your expense. Therefore, people in your life, prophet, must be identified despite what you are going through.

To know this is one thing. To identify this is to open your soul to the extent that you must know your will and your emotions and your mind to be at peace and able to deal with the unscheduled attacks in life. Samson is going through an unscheduled attack in his life. We all have seen this too many times. All prophets go through unscheduled attacks in their lives.

The reality is none of us would schedule these attacks, but over time, they build up and cause us anxiety and various forms of stress, because of who we are and whose we are. Does it always seem to you that the hard issues of life always seem to find and stay with you? Then there is the expectation for you and me, like Samson, his parents wanted him to do something else, but he did not.

The issue we must see here and see it in our personal lives is that God is speaking to Sampson through this experience, just like he is speaking to us through our issues. You can see the soul is at peace within the man during the storms of life. Like the prophet, we see Samson is maturing through this experience as he discovers the awesome power of the Holy Ghost.

This is what we must do as prophets. God is always there, but it is our soul that discovers His presence in our personal lives. The Issachar seer clearly experienced soul prosperity, and this is something every prophet must discover. The anointing of the Holy Ghost makes you deal with issues that you never wanted to speak on or touch in your personal life. You can do it because your soul is at peace. This is how we can speak the truth and be accurate.

The principle is clear. God has given His prophets the privilege and power to speak blessing upon their assignment to advance life, health, growth, joy, and self-confidence in others! We must learn to steward this privilege as a dynamic aspect of raising our mantles for this gospel's work.

The Issachar prophet's soul can be connected to the blessing we see in Numbers 6:24-26. This is the blessing God ordained over the nation of Israel. Numbers 6:24-26 (NIV) says, "The Lord bless you and keep you; the Lord make His face shine upon you, and be gracious to you; the Lord lift up His countenance upon you, and give you peace."

This fruitful blessing deserves the understanding and a conscious desire to commend its scope of goodness upon those over whom it is spoken. Imagine an Issachar prophet speaking this over your life.

The Lord bless you and keep you. The power of the spoken word is evident that the blessings of God are offered. Our God is unlimited in His capacity to prosper the efforts of those He blesses, with no restrictions. Do you want an Issachar anointed prophet to speak this upon your life?

Speak that the Lord make His face shine upon you. His face, which shines like the sun shining in its strength, will radiate His glory. Speak that glory goes before us, a glory that is beyond words as it defends from behind us, and overspreads us with the excellence of His presence (Is. 4:5; 58:8). The prophet speaking this upon your life will be because it is relevant and aligns with the will of God upon your life. Prophet, we must know that God will honor the word spoken because it is His Word. You are speaking, according to His will. Your will and the will of God are working.

The fact that the prophet is the middle person, reaching to heaven, and then to whom God directs, is an awesome wonder. The Issachar anointed prophet will minister with wisdom, faith and gentle grace that will cause those assigned to him or her to know and appreciate the call of God. The Call of God comes with much history. As an aspiring Issachar anointed prophet, we must appreciate the scriptural history of the Issachar Prophet as we strive to walk in this gift.

CHAPTER 9

HOW DO I GET THE 'ISSACHAR ANOINTING' UPON MY LIFE?

Prophets grab the mentality of getting this gift upon your life. Ask yourself as you seek it, are you really ready for it? The work needed will cost you so much of your life. So, understand that the releasing of the Issachar Anointing is prophetically released through prayer and study of God's Word. This is vital if we are to stand strong these days and to see the Kingdom advance.

Understanding and discerning the signs of the times is something to watch. We must prepare for the return of Jesus to establish His Millennial Kingdom right here on earth.

David, as Israel's King, needed an army. Men were summoned from each tribe to work with him. The men of the tribe of Issachar quickly established themselves. They were seers, able to recognize the signs of the time, and advise the King what to do.

It's this same prophetic anointing we seek to exercise today. Like David, we are convinced that this anointing needs to be released in the Church and to the nations of the world. The Issachar anointing combines insight and discernment with strategy and wisdom. The gift was necessary and proved to be quite needed.

Times and seasons are still useful and extremely important. God created this earth with seasons. Seasons allow us to experience in the natural realm of things that are also taking place in the spiritual realm.

The Issachar gift allows us to understand the created seasons strategically and specifically on earth. This is how we come to sustain life as we know it.

Many prophets are desperately seeking God right now about His plans for their lives. This is the norm as we seek God, and the key is to lay in His presence. The soaking within this gift comes upon us gradually, as we seek our purpose.

We must be aware that our specific circumstances and challenges have deterred and discouraged God's prophets because of our limited understanding of "times and seasons." Therefore, soaking and seeking God for your assignment is essential.

You will develop your inner man or spirit man by fasting to allow your inner growth. Are you determined to seek out God's plan for each new season and transition in your life, prophet? Do you want to be able to navigate the wind and the waves with clarity and focus?

The reality to experience this is that we can no longer feel and be crippled by fear of the unknown. Fear of the unknown will literally consume you, as confusion grips you. The Issachar prophet of today must learn that the spiritual senses are vital to prophetic growth.

The prophet will learn how to hear and see spiritually. The spiritual ear and spiritual eyes reveal what the Lord is saying and doing in the earth, your vision changes, and you change. Your clarity becomes exact, and your future will become brighter.

Amos 3:7 is ever so true. This prophetic Scripture is the essence of God's foundational communication with His servants, the prophets. God has always spoken to His prophets and people through "times and seasons."

Prophets here is what you must know. Often when God is revealing His agenda it is so easy to forget we are only a part of a bigger picture. When we do not see our agenda, that's a distraction.

The focus on our bumps in the road make us lose sight of God's goals and perspectives. Welcome to moment by moment, this thing called life, prophet.

It is important to maintain our scope and remember that there is an end goal. Look at this example. We see the sons of Issachar were able to totally commit themselves to David. They understood that it was time for God to fulfill His prophetic word given by Samuel 17 years earlier (1 Sam. 15:28).

This experience needs to be understood. The Lord granted them a special anointing. They understood the prophetic timing for when He would tear the kingdom of Israel away from rebellious Saul. God would give it over to His servant David (1 Sam. 15:22-28).

Can you imagine that? This gift provides a history of insight. This does not happen with your soul, not in agreement. We see a prophet with total submission and willing to follow what God said to the letter, and they were additionally rewarded.

The Issachar anointed prophet was a forerunner of a renewed kingdom that was built on obedience to God instead of rebellion and sin. The gift brought them honor and prosperity, and you must understand that they were not our front, it was David .

The issue of us being the End-Time Sons of Issachar will be continued to be debated long after you have read this book multiple times. We have approached the age of difficult times. The prophets of today must become more like the Issachar seer in his or her capacity to understand the times and know what to do.

We want the Issachar anointing. We need to pray and believe that the Issachar anointing would be released upon the prophets who desire it. We must speak and believe in our worldwide influence to understand the times and know what to do.

Genesis 49:14-15 was Jacob's prophecy over Issachar. These Scriptures say, "Issachar is a strong donkey, lying down between the sheepfolds. When he saw that a resting place was good and that the land was pleasant, he bowed his shoulder to bear burdens, and became a slave at forced labor."

To receive the "Sons of Issachar" anointing means you are able to bear burdens. You can handle the pressure of the gift. The prophet is one of the most valuable gifts of the body of Christ. The gift is needed for the times we are entering.

Read that again. We need to remind ourselves of this fact as those tough times show up, again and again.

The prophets of today, must be multi-dimensional. We must strive to operate in the boldness of Judah. We must have an awareness of Issachar, with the revelation of Zebulun. They will therefore be well-equipped to fulfill God's purpose for their lives and fulfill the life assignments of Gods' plan.

There is no doubt that serious spirits will attempt in a very pronounced way to hinder the last day church. We all know that. These are always going to be grumblers, fault finders, and followers after their own lusts. There are just a few I will name, but we all have experienced them and their cousins of drama (Jude 1:11-16).

So again, let us ask how do I get this anointing upon me? I seek it with everything I have inside. While I did not mention the soul very much, it was the central theme of the entire chapter. My will can do it. My mind will focus for such extreme training and I will not quit this type of training when everything around me says quit.

Those of you who really want to be Issachar trained anointed prophets, must understand that the mentality is the start. Your soul is central and the center of everything you do or do not do. Reread this chapter again for some specific keys to allow this gift to fall upon your mantle. Finally, understanding the Issachar history will inspire and help you appreciate the Issachar gift.

CHAPTER 10

HISTORY OF THE ISSACHAR ANOINTING

1 Chronicles 12:32 says, "And of the children of Issachar, which were men that had an understanding of the times, to know what Israel ought to do; the heads of them were two hundred; and all their brethren were at their commandment." They were prophets/seers who knew how to ascertain the periods of the sun and moon, the intercalation of months, the dates of solemn feasts, and could interpret the signs of the times.

Have you ever dealt with a period when you had to leave your comfort zone and deal with the burden of the process in prophetic ministry? You needed someone sent by God to speak into your life, someone who knew God and could steer and direct you. You needed someone gifted and processing the "sons of Issachar" anointing to know the times and what you and God's people should do except in a very general sense.

Who is Issachar? Let us look at some history of this special gifting. As we see, Issachar is the ninth son of his father Jacob/Israel and the fifth son of his mother, Leah. The Scripture tells us that just before Jacob/Israel died, he called his sons together.

Each son got a personal message, which was like a prophecy of what would befall them in the future days. Genesis 49:1 says, "And Jacob called unto his sons, and said, gather yourselves together, that I may tell you that which shall befall you in the last days."

Jacob is near death, and he speaks his final words to Issachar. Genesis 49:14-15 says, "Issachar is a strong ass couching down between two burdens: And he saw that rest was good, and the land that it was pleasant; and bowed his shoulder to bear, and became a servant unto tribute."

Clearly, the gift is not defined by his name, but by the word spoken over him by his father. Jacob in his utterance is positioning his son Issachar as a backbone that other leaders would stand on and be blessed.

Many today express the Issachar gift that represents a skeletal system. Throughout history, this gift would be a gift of fire that many leaders would stand on and be empowered and blessed.

Genesis 30:14-18 and other Scriptures mention this very gifted group of prophets mainly in the background of other well-known ministries. Issachar provides the spiritual skeletal system works in the background, supporting and bearing the weight of leadership support, which is essential if the body of Christ is to function properly.

As you come to understand the Issachar gift more, it will become like a system of prophets and seers who support leaders. They are the backbones of ministries. They are the skilled prophetic voices of the time: current and future.

The prophets are more often behind the scenes. They are never exposed or visible. So gifted and yet you may never know who they are because they serve to live, and they live to serve. The 'Issachar Anointing' does not always have to be out front to work effectively.

Issachar's knowledge of astronomy and mathematics was evident as they had the understanding of what Israel ought to do. What is amazing is that there were only about 200 prophets who were directly anointed in this gift. We do see that this number grew, so we know that there are opportunities for those who will seek this anointing. James 1:5 says, "If any of you lack wisdom, let him ask of God, that giveth to all men liberally, and upbraideth not; and it shall be given him."

As we look at their knowledge of the gift of discernment, these are only a few reasons why the Issachar gift benefitted those they were assigned to serve. The gift was a gift that developed other gifts.

The sons of Issachar today would be like those who blessed and provided for others. The Issachar gift is a prophetic and apostolic gift sent to make a difference in other people's lives. 1 Chronicles 7:5 says, "And their brethren among all the families of Issachar were valiant men of might, reckoned in all by their genealogies fourscore and seven thousand.', those of the tribe of Issachar are also shown to be valiant men of might."

This type of anointing is needed today. God still honors this gift today. Those who possess it become spiritual farmers for others to graze in the prepared fields. There is a noticed benefit for all who will open themselves to the wisdom of the Issachar gift. In other words, what you're growing is providing opportunities for others to grow.

Your utterance, ministry, and assignments are the fields changing lives for Christ. God provided all good things to all who were poor and oppressed and needed this gift.

Can you imagine being so gifted that your knowledge and understanding of the times would make you the keepers of the biblical calendar? Many came to understand the duly appointed times and seasons of when Israel should observe specific feasts of the Lord (Lev. 23).

The Lord's Feasts symbolically reveal God's plan and timing of His redemption. The Issachar Prophets had an anointing, which gave them a unique insight into God's timing of things past, present, and future. Clearly, they were seers with a special anointing.

Deuteronomy 33:18-19 sheds light on the 'Issachar Anointing' developing financial servanthood. The Scriptures say the sons of Issachar drew out the abundance of the sea and the hidden treasures of the sand. God called them, His Issachar prophets. These specially gifted prophets were to provide food to the whole of Israel. They were as an "indentured servant" to their brethren among the other tribes (Gen. 19:14-15).

In Deuteronomy 27:12, we see spiritual servanthood as we study the Issachar gift. They "excelled in the words of the law, and were endued with wisdom, and were obedient to their command." Their knowledge of God's Word caused them to become the primary cultivators of Israel's spiritual treasures, and their counsel and interpretations of Scripture were received as authoritative.

One of the most profound works of the Issachar gift is seen in Judges 5:15, which says, "And the princes of Issachar were with Deborah; even Issachar, and Barak: he was sent on foot into the valley." Prophetess Deborah was looked upon very highly by the Issachar tribe.

The days of the Prophetess Deborah were a time when men dominated the culture. We see Prophetess Deborah as a judge, wife, and functioning in the prophetic office all at the same time. She symbolized the importance of the law in Israel and was a key figure because of the Issachar influence. Thus, we see the institution of sexism eliminated by the anointing.

History has really hyped on the fact of Issachar's patient and quiet strength. We should not take the Issachar anointing sometimes as weak, just because we may fail to understand it. The discernment of this prophetic gift is a standard and a level that will require work for us to obtain. Our hunger should be fueled by our lack of understanding of exactly how God may choose to use an Issachar Prophet.

There needs to be known that there is no weakness in God. The weakness is in us. Therefore, we must get our soul connected and open to God's plan. Our prosperity in this gift starts with soul prosperity.

Ancient Israel, where we see this gift initially introduced, is destined for physical and spiritual prosperity. The Issachar were mighty men of valor who God used to serve other tribes, nations and perform the difficult tasks needed to help bring them closer to Himself.

1 Chronicles 7:1-5 says, "Now the sons of Issachar were, Tola, and Puah, Jashub, and Shimrom, four. 2 And the sons of Tola; Uzzi, and Rephaiah, and Jeriel, and Jahmai, and Jibsam, and Shemuel, heads of their father's house, to wit, of Tola: they were valiant men of might in their generations; whose number was in the days of David two and twenty thousand and six hundred. 3 And the sons of Uzzi; Izrahiah: and the sons of Izaiah; Michael, and Obadiah, and Joel, Ishiah, five: all of them chief men. 4 And with them, by their generations, after the house of their fathers, were bands of soldiers for war, six and thirty thousand men: for they had many wives and sons. 5 And

their brethren among all the families of Issachar were valiant men of might, reckoned in all by their genealogies fourscore and seven thousand."

This is the history of the Issachar Prophets. Let us combine and join to work on ourselves to achieve this level of gifting for the total work of the Kingdom of God.

Blessings
Apostle Ken Cox

ABOUT THE AUTHOR

Apostle Ken Cox started serving God in 1994 after a series of unforeseen life failures. Out of the military and seemly starting life over again, by 2000, Apostle Cox had found his life calling as a Prophet. The challenge of learning and understanding presented a new frontier. Apostle Cox dove into the process and has now emerged as a well-traveled prophet who serves the Body of Christ as an Apostle.

Apostle Cox, along with his wife, Prophetess Sabina Cox are the leaders of Where Eagles Fly Fellowship Inc., a fellowship of prophets and apostle across the USA and beyond who are dedicated and focused on establishing the prophetic gift back into society as they raise up prophets around the country and abroad.

Apostle Cox and Prophetess Cox are available for Revivals, Conferences and Meetings. They have been featured in meetings and sought-after to teach and instruct the prophetic for ministries seeking to learn more about the gift. Apostle and Prophetess Cox have 3 children and 4 grandkids as of this writing and currently reside in Durham, NC. Contact them through the Where Eagles Fly office at 919-695-3375 or 919-213-1328 or at www.whereeaglesfly.us.

INDEX

5

5-fold ministry gifts, 4

A

Aaron, 52, 66
Abraham, 72, 73
abundance, 18, 34, 89
accuracy, 49, 50, 57
Amalekites, 62, 63, 65, 66, 67
angels,, 51
anointed, 31, 34, 49, 50, 51, 52, 56, 76, 77, 82, 84, 88
anointing, 11, 26, 29, 32, 33, 34, 43, 45, 46, 47, 48, 51, 53, 54, 55, 56, 61, 72, 75, 79, 81, 82, 83, 86, 88, 89, 90, 91
Apostles, 4, 68
aspiring prophets, 2
attacks, 6, 9, 65, 74

B

Bethsaida, 30, 31
blind, 8, 20, 28, 29, 30, 31, 32, 33, 34
blocked, 7, 10
Body of Christ, 17, 18, 46, 58, 59, 93
boldness, 83
bondage, 38, 59, 61
breakthrough, 8, 57, 73
breakthrough anointing, 8
broken place, 10
burdens, 48, 82, 83, 86

C

children, 1, 9, 45, 46, 65, 85, 94
Christianity, 22
comfort zone, 85
commitment, 11
communication, 10, 26, 80
communion, 16
confusion, 6, 66, 80
counsel, 19, 90

D

David, 62, 79, 81, 82, 91
demonic operations, 10

destiny, 2, 31, 39, 40, 44
development, 1, 11, 25, 41, 44, 51, 55, 56, 57
discern, 3, 21, 26
discerning, 10, 78
discernment, 26, 47, 49, 56, 57, 79, 88, 91
discipline, 19, 48
dishonor, 8
dreams, 40

E

emotions, 4, 5, 6, 8, 9, 11, 12, 14, 18, 22, 33, 43, 50, 56, 58, 70, 73, 74
empowered, 1, 2, 20, 26, 87
End-Time, 82
enemy, 7, 10, 11, 20, 44, 59, 61, 62, 65, 66, 67, 68, 73
Eschatology, 15, 57, 58, 59

F

faith, 11, 15, 21, 45, 52, 66, 74, 77
family, 9, 40, 60
fast, 22, 23, 24, 25, 57
fasting, 22, 24, 25, 26, 80
fear, 8, 18, 25, 49, 62, 80
fight of faith, 52
finances, 9, 12
focus, 1, 2, 23, 25, 26, 33, 63, 80, 81, 84

free moral agents, 17
fruit, 16, 17

G

generation, 1, 46, 49, 67
generational lineage, 64
glory, 29, 76
God's hand, 54
God's timing, 54, 89
god-children, 9
gospel's work, 75
grandchildren, 9

H

health, 5, 6, 9, 11, 12, 42, 43, 75
heart, 4, 5, 10, 15, 41, 45
heavenly encounters, 22, 51
Holy of Holies, 14, 16
hope, 29
hopelessness, 40

I

Inner Court, 14
inner man, 13, 14, 15, 16, 17, 19, 80
Israel, 17, 24, 47, 48, 59, 63, 66, 75, 79, 81, 85, 86, 87, 89, 90, 91

Issachar gifting, 29, 54
Issachar Seer, 1, 2, 18, 20, 21, 23, 39, 44, 51, 52, 57
Issachar Seer., 1, 18, 44

J

Jehoshaphat, 24, 25
Jesus, 7, 9, 15, 25, 26, 29, 30, 31, 32, 33, 34, 36, 41, 52, 68, 69, 78
Joshua, 66, 67
joy, 5, 7, 8, 75
judge, 30, 34, 35, 54, 90

K

Kingdom of Heaven, 20
knowledge, 4, 6, 26, 38, 39, 44, 45, 46, 48, 56, 87, 88, 89, 90

L

leaders, 1, 8, 26, 48, 56, 72, 86, 87, 93
love, 2, 5, 14, 18

M

mantle, 1, 26, 49, 50, 84
meditate, 10

Melchizedek, 72
mentality level, 72
mentor, 34, 36
messages, 10
Millennial Kingdom, 78
mind, 4, 6, 9, 11, 12, 14, 15, 17, 18, 19, 21, 23, 33, 42, 44, 46, 50, 51, 58, 70, 74, 84
ministers of Christ, 5
miracles, 28, 33
Moses, 13, 14, 15, 16, 17, 18, 19, 66, 67, 68
mysteries., 5

N

nations, 8, 47, 48, 79, 91

O

obedience, 16, 44, 71, 82
Outer Court, 14, 16

P

peers, 8, 34, 35, 54
persecuted, 10
physical hunger, 23, 24
physical senses, 21, 23, 50
power, 17, 26, 29, 39, 40, 41, 66, 71, 72, 75, 76
preaching, 8

problem, 7, 8, 9, 18, 59
Process of Senses Enlightenment, 22
prophecy, 17, 19, 82, 86
Prophet, 6, 7, 8, 9, 11, 13, 16, 17, 18, 21, 24, 27, 28, 29, 30, 34, 37, 42, 51, 57, 58, 67, 76, 77, 91, 93
Prophetess Deborah, 90
prophetic block, 29, 35, 36
Prophetic DNA, 74
prophetic mentors, 8
prophetic ministry, 17, 85
prophetic movement, 2
prophetic office, 2, 90
prophetic readers, 2
prophetic utterance, 48
Prosperity, 5, 12, 46
purposes of God, 1

R

reaching, 36, 39, 40, 77
redemption., 89
rejection, 49
revelation, 3, 6, 19, 21, 29, 49, 56, 83
righteous, 7, 15, 54

S

Sampson, 74
Samuel, 5, 36, 62, 65, 81

Saul, 62, 63, 64, 81

secret, 25, 28

seer anointing, 20

seers, 1, 2, 20, 33, 38, 40, 45, 47, 51, 52, 53, 54, 60, 79, 85, 87, 89

Seers, 4, 11, 19, 22, 25, 26, 38, 40, 43, 44, 50, 51

skeletal system, 87

sons of Issachar, 81, 88, 89, 91

soul, 1, 2, 3, 4, 5, 6, 7, 8, 9, 10, 11, 12, 13, 14, 15, 16, 17, 18, 19, 20, 22, 23, 24, 25, 27, 28, 29, 31, 32, 35, 37, 38, 39, 40, 41, 42, 43, 44, 45, 50, 53, 57, 58, 61, 64, 65, 67, 68, 70, 72, 74, 75, 81, 83, 84, 91

soul issues, 7

sphere of influence, 20

Spirit, 6, 8, 10, 11, 17, 19, 21, 22, 25, 26, 32, 38, 43, 51, 73

spirit realm, 20

spiritual children, 9

spiritual hunger, 23

spiritual senses, 21, 50, 51, 80

Spiritual warfare, 6

spouse, 9

stewards, 5

strongholds, 8, 9, 37, 38, 39, 40, 42, 43, 44, 46

Study, 39

submission, 6, 9, 15, 17

supernatural, 20, 26, 51, 55

supernatural realm, 20

T

teaching, 8, 22, 39
Tent of Testimony, 14
testimony, 14, 16
thief, 9, 10
times and seasons, 1, 47, 49, 80, 81, 89
torment, 58, 61, 67, 68
tribe of Issachar, 79, 88
true unity, 14
trust, 53, 54, 61, 70

U

understanding of the times, 47, 85, 89
unteachable, 7

V

visions, 22, 40, 51
voice, 26, 56, 62

W

Watchmen, 4
wilderness, 14, 60
will, 1, 2, 4, 5, 6, 7, 8, 9, 10, 11, 12, 14, 15, 16, 17, 18, 19, 20, 21, 22, 23, 24, 25, 26, 27, 29, 30, 31, 32, 33, 34, 35, 38, 39, 40, 41, 43, 44, 45, 47, 49, 50, 52,

53, 54, 55, 56, 57, 58, 59, 60, 61, 62, 66, 67, 68, 70, 72, 73, 74, 76, 77, 78, 80, 82, 83, 84, 87, 88, 91
  wisdom, 19, 26, 42, 47, 54, 55, 71, 77, 79, 88, 90
  Wisdom, 4
  Word, 5, 6, 7, 8, 9, 12, 16, 23, 39, 41, 42, 46, 70, 76, 78, 90

www.ingramcontent.com/pod-product-compliance
Lightning Source LLC
Chambersburg PA
CBHW052110110526
44592CB00013B/1558